THINK AGAIN AND GROW RICH

What the rich know that we
don't know

Henry McCarthy

©Copyright

All rights reserved. No part of this publication may be reproduced, distributed, or transmitted in any form or by any means, including photocopying, recording, or other electronic or mechanical methods, without the prior written permission of the publisher, except in the case of brief quotations embodied in critical reviews and certain other noncommercial uses permitted by copyright law.

Copywrite © Henry McCarthy, 2022

Table of Contents

Introduction

Section I

Chapter 1

Chapter 2

Chapter 3

SECTION II

Chapter 4

Chapter 5

Section III

Chapter 6

SUMMARY

Introduction

The mentality of a millionaire is a great thing, and something we all desired we knew more about and how to obtain one. Knowing what the affluent (Rich) people believe when it comes to success, wealth, money and the world totally would undoubtedly educate everyone. Knowledge will always be power. Being rich or poor is a mindset. It all starts from the brain. What the rich know that the poor don't know makes the difference. That is the reason of this pic of work. To emphasis on what the rich know that the average or poor man need to think over again and become as rich as he desires. But of all these. There is normally one thing the affluent and the regular person are constantly worrying about which is MONEY. We all assume we know about money. But do we comprehend the purposes of money what money truly is, and what it represents? How and when did the first money appear? Do we conceive of it as a means to quantify value? Is it a reliable store of value? Who truly makes the money we use? Is it a commodity to be traded? And how does this money genuinely connect to our position, to the true worth of items we use in our lives, to the work we make to attain them, to the real economics of human settlements?. My objective is not to teach you something you have never heard successful people say before; it is to show you something worth thinking over again if you are ready to become wealthy.

Section I

Chapter 1

What the rich know that we don't know

As stated. Knowing what the wealthy think is always really intriguing to the one who wishes to become one of the rich and succesful. I take satisfaction in unearthing opinions about the rich that are somewhat underrated, what they genuinely believe about the world, and how they came to be where they are. But one interesting thing is that the rich are always thinking about what made them what they are, which is money, and how to maintain where they are or even earn more.

How do you think the wealthy looked at money?. They see money as a social technology, not a physical thing. Once you start thinking about them, they are highly slippery questions, ones that have puzzled many throughout the millennia. mostly because the remedy seems so apparent. Is it not the penny in your pocket, the dollar bill in its clip, the credit card in your wallet, the check in the mail, or the electrical impulse in the computer? Money is all things, but none of them, since money is a technique for ordering our lives. But in a specific, arbitrary way: an attempt to neatly fit the constantly ambiguous qualities of our experience into numbers—quantities that can be counted and compared to traditional units of account, where everything is measured against a monetary sum.

"Money" is the operating system on which we run our economies. The issue is that money is not a material at all but a social technology: a set of ideas and practices that control what we generate and consume as well as the way we live together. When it comes to money itself—rather than the symbols that represent it, the account books where people record it, or the facilities such as banks in which people manage it—there is nothing concrete to look at… But currency is not money in and of itself. Coins and money, in other words, are valued tokens to record the underlying system of credit accounts and conduct the underlying process of clearing.

Unfortunately, when we think of money, we automatically think of coins or precious metals, not of an organization through which a process of trust is managed. We should not focus on what money is, but on what it does. The main fact about its existence is that money is a strategy, or approach, established to manage trust… trust that a creditor would be repaid. One may say that is the operating system on which we run our economy. This book is written after a deep examination and with information about what the rich think and do that the average person needs to think over again.

The rich don't view money in terms of what it can buy. The rich think differently about money. The ordinary mind concentrates on the things money can buy every time the problem of money comes up. This is why people are usually astonished by how much money the ultra-rich have.

You will see the average mind thinking about the accessories of the rich, such as "what can they acquire with that amount of money?" But that inquiry is one of the reasons why such a rich situation is difficult for them. When rich people see money, they don't notice things. The rich consider money as power. The rich regard money as a remote control, as a tool. This is why they have billions and still persist in the game. Meanwhile, the usual person would retire and take a vacation for the rest of their lives on $30 million. A wealthy person in this sense is a person who has the capacity to earn at least $1 million in the span of a year if they lose everything today. Probably You've met those types of people.

15 Surprising Ways Rich People Think Differently.

Rich folks don't think like regular people. That's the world we live in.

Being able to retain a big fortune over a lengthy period of time is not anything simple if you don't have the appropriate attitude. How would you explain why a high proportion of lottery winners become bankrupt within a few years? They don't have the rich people attitude.

When you look at the way rich individuals think, you will see some surprising commonalities. Here are 15 unexpected methods the rich think:

1. They think about themselves first.
Before contributing big quantities of money to organizations, they make sure they benefit themselves first. They did not grow rich and remain rich by assisting people recklessly. When they do anything, they

know what's in it for them. It's not selfishness, it's remaining rich.

2. They are continuously thinking about the future.
The future is merely the present waiting to happen. Wealthy individuals recognize that if they want to retain their lifestyle, they have to think for the long term. Globalization, financial crises, and international wars represent opportunities or hazards for the rich person. Not exploiting long-term possibilities and dismissing prospective dangers is a prescription for becoming mediocre.

3. They are action-oriented.
They don't simply relax and wait for interest to trickle in. In an ever-changing environment, rich individuals think about the future yet have the resources to act today. Good investors know how to make a

swift choice to capture a fleeting opportunity.

4. They are enthusiastic.
Their hobbies might differ, but rich individuals have the money and the leisure to satisfy their passions. If they don't want to do anything, they can always hire someone else to do it for them and then spend more time shooting deer if that's what they enjoy.

5. They favor particular knowledge over conventional schooling.
Since they are action-oriented, they choose an education that serves a tangible aim. Education is crucial, but being outstanding in a specialized field is more important. Rich individuals get exceedingly rich by being good at doing something or at doing something nobody has dared to undertake. College drop-outs pursuing their start-up aspirations to become millionaires are a long-lasting cliché, but the fact is that

gaining particular skills early on will offer them an advantage.

6. They are wildly ambitious.
And they need to be. If they were not, they would settle with "richer than average." Very rich individuals will never be content with the quantity of riches they have. They have an internal compass that points towards "more money," which implies greater initiatives.

7. They are not frightened to invest.
Rich individuals have been presented with innumerable get-rich-quick hoaxes, and they know what it takes to get where they are: work, time, or money. Since they came to a place where the largest leverage they have is money, and that's what they have more of than the others, they realize they will have to invest to earn. You win some, you lose some.

8. They know how to leverage other people's money.

Even if they have a lot of money, they know how to utilize other people's money to achieve what they want. Bank loans, strategic partnerships... a global perspective will help them to find other people's money to make their investment profitable.

9. They surround themselves with like-minded individuals.

Having the lifestyle of rich people is quite peculiar... they don't have the same hobbies as ordinary people, and there are not many individuals with whom you can share your anxieties about having to pay millions in income taxes. They will flock together in similar groupings and love being together wherever in the globe.

10. They pick the best personnel.

They recognize that their success resides with the individuals who work for them. Rich individuals know what they want, have very little time for administrative work, and depend significantly on their staff. Since there is a lot at risk, they will choose the best and pay appropriately.

11. They can seize everyone up in an instant.
Rich individuals are constantly approached by regular people, who always come to beg them for anything. After a period, it becomes easier for them to judge others. It's a question of practice!

12. They have a highly accurate detector.
They will ask a few questions, but they will learn a lot from you. Since they have a global view, they will challenge your recommendations with their experience or outside-the-box comparisons. They will detect if you are feigning knowledge, even if they don't know your subject.

13. They don't care about what you think of them.

They don't have anything to prove anymore. They won't feel the need to show off their money or exhibit any type of status. They will be extremely discreet in revealing that they belong to a higher socioeconomic level.

14. They think of the world as a little place.
The super-wealthy are not trapped in a certain nation. They are purchasing the nicest properties throughout the globe and see the world as being a little place. Being in three different nations in one day is not strange for them, and they will get a sense of where the world's pulse is.

15. They raise their children to be rich. Their offspring will manage a great wealth as well. It is truly a depressing scenario to think that your children would dilapidate the money you or your parents earned with hard effort. They will strive to educate their children

about the worth of money so that they learn to take nothing for granted. The wise rich don't give their children what they want rather they let them work for it or pay a fee for it to make sure they grasp the worth of the transaction.

Chapter 2

Habits and Things Rich People Do

Building a habit is one easy thing to attempt. Building it could be a bit challenging. But suppose you fell through with it. It becomes an effortless habit for you. Here are 10 distinct habits of the rich:

1. They get out of debt. Duh, right? Debt is the adversary of developing wealth. Debt is Lord Voldemort. It will kill you and ruin your money. You should get rid of even small monthly payments. Start by finding out precisely how much you owe, then pick what you're going to handle first.

2. They know how much they save. Do you know what your yearly savings rate is? Rich folks do. It doesn't have to be accurate or down to the cent, but you should know how

much of your paycheck you generally save or invest.

3. They know how much they spend. How much are your monthly utilities? How much do you generally spend at restaurants? By finding out these things, you will be able to identify strategies to save and invest more. So, monitor your expenditures over the following few months. After you've seen where your money is going, you will have a better notion of what you can trim.

4. They think long-term. Where do you want to be in 5, 10, or 20 years? Wherever it is, you need to start preparing for it now. Rich individuals don't say things like, "I want new shoes. I'm going to spend the rest of my money on them." They think long-term about where they want to go, and they establish financial goals to get there.

5. They make their money work for them. My dream is to discover a way to generate

money while I sleep. Doesn't it sound amazing? Well, affluent people do that. They invest in stocks, real estate, businesses, etc., and make their money work for them instead of them working for the money.

6. They diversify their income. Nothing will make you feel safer at work than having another source of income, and it will assist your bank account, too. Having a few side hustles will help your bank account grow—and it will offer you less time to spend your money, which improves your savings.

7. They aren't frightened to receive assistance. It may be your brother, your sister, or even your best friend's parents, but you should select someone who you believe manages money effectively, and ask them how they do it. Also, there are a ton of amazing Internet resources you can check out. In addition, you may go to financial planners and find out what they propose.

You're probably not going to discover all your answers in one area, and that's great. Just keep looking until you discover something that works for you.

8. They establish clear objectives for their money. You need objectives. You need something to aspire toward at every phase of your financial path. Are you working on getting out of debt? Then you should have a large "get out of debt goal." You should also split down your major goal into smaller components. For example, "pay off a credit card, pay off $5,000 in school debts, or pay off half of your car." By creating these minor objectives, you will remain motivated to reach your greater goal.

9. They recognize that becoming rich is a process. It's not going to happen quickly, but by developing a strategy and sticking with it, you will ultimately get there.

10. They don't desire what other people have. Do you know the couple with the

magnificent house? Do you know the gal with the great car? Most of them aren't affluent. They may have decent earnings, but they're most likely buried in payments. Trying to attain these things will make you feel the same way. You will be buried in payments, but you won't be making progress on your net worth. Decide what you desire more: riches or things.

Chapter 3

How The Rich View And perceive Money.

Here are 7 ways the rich perceive money differently:

1. The rich perceive money as a person. When average people think about money, they think about what to sell to acquire it. But the rich concentrate on people with money. In their perspective, money symbolizes individuals.

Think about it; all the money in the world is under the control of someone. If you can convince a person to open their hands, you obtain what they have. The average mentality goes after the money in the hands of individuals. The rich go for the people. This is because they understand that if they win over the people, they will receive the money.

In the sight of the rich, sacks of money stroll by them on the street every day. They don't regard individuals as money. But they regard money as an individual.

2. The rich perceive money as a complement (and not a rival) to time. The normal mind that goes through education thinks of money as a reward for labor and time invested. The rich don't. This is why the rich don't hunt for places to make money in return for time. The rich will rather seek out places to beg for money and receive it.

Money complements time. Money makes time fun. However, really rich individuals would never exchange their time for money. They spend their time following their aspirations and accomplishing work that provides them satisfaction.

The typical person attempts to find satisfaction in the sale of time for money. and it is a fight. This is why rich people can work 20 hours a day and not grumble. They didn't choose what they do because of the promise of financial remuneration for their time.

3. The rich don't feel cheated when others take advantage of them financially. This is a vision of money that is quite challenging for average people. Rich individuals readily ignore it when other people take advantage of them. Not that they don't pay attention, but they are typically relaxed, knowing they will likely utilize that to acquire favor.

Many times, individuals who take advantage of the frugality of the rich do not react in kind when the tables turn. This finally kills the relationship. And the wealthy use it to end unproductive relationships.

The rich won't quarrel with you when you cheat them. But if you cannot be beneficial to them when it is most necessary, you may have to say goodbye to the relationship. They consider money as a tool, and so they are not emotional to the degree of yelling at someone attempting to take some coins.

4. The rich regard money in terms of what it is going to generate. If you owe a rich guy $1 million, he won't be furious because of the $1 million. Instead, he will be upset because of what that $1 million would have turned into if he had it.

Rich individuals are continually looking at the future worth of what they have. The current value is only applicable when there is an imminent transaction to be made. What actually matters to the rich is what the value of their money will look like in the future.

5. The rich consider money as a weapon to control perception. To the rich, perception is reality. A lot of rich individuals take their perception seriously. Perception is how others view you. Regular people frequently depend on the natural flow of life to construct their perspective, whereas rich individuals are often proactive about this.

Using money to develop perception is not restricted to costly attire, expensive parties, and the like. In reality, some live extremely humble lifestyles. However, they create the appropriate noise with their charities, contributions, and accomplishment reports. Rich individuals strive especially hard in this area to be liked by common people. This is because being neutral will be a problem when there is an issue of negative publicity. If they don't work hard to establish a favorable impression of themselves, someone might wake up one morning and portray them in the worst conceivable light. And they might lose a lot of good fortune and money before they get the opportunity to put the record right.

To the rich, money is a weapon to mold public opinion.

6. The rich consider money as the actual manifestation of people's interests. Here is an innovative technique to evaluate public interest in any product (or service) you are working on: Show it to others. Ask whether they enjoy it. Then ask if they would be

prepared to pay 10 times what you expect to charge for it.

Of course, the response will likely be a no, but what you should look out for is how they give you the no. Those who offer (by themselves) a sum they can pay for the answer are those who are actually interested in the solution.

An interest that is not paired with money is not a true interest. It is only a simple desire. When individuals can exchange their hard-earned dollars for it, it is a genuine measure of interest. Rich individuals have mastered this.

7. The rich perceive money as an efficient weapon to purchase other people's time. The rich create more time for themselves by purchasing time from individuals ready to exchange it. This is not a negative thing on both ends. It is only an issue of necessity. The rich have money but need time. And there is someone who has time and needs money.

Money is a terrific instrument to attract time and talent to your camp. There are plenty of individuals in the world who won't be working on what they are working on if they are not compensated. Money is tremendously important for purchasing time and skill.

There are additional ways the rich understand money, but I think they are significant enough to begin you thinking in the correct direction.
If you want to be rich, don't work for money. Let money work for you.

SECTION II

Chapter 4

What The Rich Believe About Being wealthy.

The best way to get rich is not in the mechanics of money but in the degree of thinking that creates it.

In addition to possessing higher financial account balances than average, rich individuals have diverse views, ideologies, and techniques.

There are numerous ways the rich view the world differently from ordinary people. Number eight is highlighted below.

1. Rich individuals believe being affluent is a right, whereas the average person considers wealth to be a luxury.

World-class intellectuals realize in a capitalist economy they have the right to be rich if they're ready to produce huge value for others."

The bulk thinks being rich is reserved for a fortunate few. This divide in thinking sends the middle class to the lottery and the global class to work, They [the affluent] believe if they make life better or easier for others, it's their right to be rich.

2. Rich individuals believe establishing a company is the quickest method to generate money, while the typical person believes starting a business is dangerous.

The reality is, that having a job is no safer than running a company or business. As contradictory as this may sound, those who work for themselves have the freedom to aggressively seek new business and boost profits at will.

Of course, there are dangers associated with launching a company, but affluent individuals recognize the biggest risk is not betting on themselves.

While rich individuals create enterprises and benefit from them, regular people settle for a constant wage and so lose out on the possibility to build a fortune. People practically guarantee themselves a life of financial mediocrity by sticking with a job that pays a reasonable wage and provides regular raises.

3. Rich individuals believe the affluent are more sophisticated, while the typical person believes the wealthy are smarter.
If the secret to acquiring money was high marks in school, every Cambridge College graduate would be rich. Amassing money has more to do with street smarts than your capacity to recall facts and thrive on tests.
How do you become savvier? Get into the thoughts of those who are already rich, and find out what they think and believe about money.

4. Rich individuals believe developing money involves a team. whereas the

ordinary person feels that generating money is an individual endeavor.

The global class realizes it takes a team to develop wealth, and they invest most of their time in recruiting the appropriate individuals to amplify their actions and ideas. The greatest fortunes are produced by the collaborative mental and physical efforts of a world-class team.

He thinks that who you surround yourself with has more of an influence on your net worth than you may think.

5. Rich individuals believe generating money is straightforward. While the normal person believes creating money is complex,

The public has always felt that rich individuals are wiser, luckier, or better educated. Of course, none of these things are true.

The rich recognize that money flows from ideas and problem resolution. The greater the answer, the higher the payout. Making money may not be easy, but it is simple.

There is no secret about becoming rich, yet this restrictive notion keeps most people from ever attempting it.

6. Rich individuals believe money is obtained via thought, while the average person thinks money is earned through time and exertion.
The middle class considers money in linear terms, whereas the wealthy consider money in non-linear terms. The rich know that creative thinking is the highest-paid ability in the world. Training your intellect to discover answers to complex issues is the actual key to producing money.

7. Rich individuals believe money is freeing, while the normal person believes money is controlling.
The rich perceive money as a good weapon that has the capacity to generate freedom and opportunity for themselves and their family.

By contrast, the common individual perceives money as "the great oppressor." While the global class sees money as a crucial resource that opens up unlimited possibilities, the middle class is denouncing it and rejecting its usefulness. With a worldview like this, is it any surprise most people don't have much?

8. Rich individuals believe in working for satisfaction, while the common person believes in working for money.
The rich have long realized that working with the sole aim of generating money is the poorest technique for creating wealth.
Don't hunt for employment with the largest compensation potential, rather concentrate on work that has the most satisfaction potential. Once you discover it, pour so much heart and soul into your profession that you become one of the most skilled people in your area. You'll be rewarded with exceptional fortune.

Secrets Rich People Won't Tell You About Their Habits and Lives

They don't go to the ATM every day. They withdraw once in a while and pay for anything they require with cash. That way, they're compelled to keep to a budget without counting pennies or collecting receipts. They can spend just what is in their wallet.

They don't squander as much as you think. Most of the top rich guys barely spend on stuff that won't yield earnings. They don't spend on obligations and luxuries. They perceive things this way Not spending money is the same as earning money. So if I save $2,000 by not traveling first class, that's the same as someone giving me $2,000! Wouldn't you stay in an uncomfortable chair for three hours for $2,000? —a successful Boston plastic sit and those are some clever money-saving ideas you probably haven't considered before.

They don't quite obtain it until they obtain the agreement. Perseverance is one of their traits. They continue to do whatever they believe will get them what they want. It's not always simple, but you see that it is done.
They are not as brilliant as we think. Yes. Rich individuals do take selfish actions that don't pay off in the end. They make ridiculous actions occasionally that only dumb ones will do. But one thing they don't do is stay stuck in their errors. They always come back.

They tolerate risks to attain success. The wealthy pursue greater goals than are physically possible, and great risks are usually associated with the cost. Sometimes it seems silly. But to them, it appears good.

Chapter 5

DIFFERENCE BETWEEN THE RICH MINDSET AND THE POOR MINDSET

The Rich versus Poor Mindset: The point is that overlooking excellence, becoming a perpetual learner, and cautious risk management are all variations between the rich and poor. This minimizes their possibility of becoming destitute once tragedy hits, and it helps them reach their financial objectives over the long run.

A rich mindset will tell you to be self-sufficient and generate many sources of income. It will advise you to develop a team of wiser individuals than yourself to utilize the work of brilliant people. The mindset of the rich is the most crucial reason why "the rich keep becoming wealthier, while the poor become poorer." Bill Gates has been cited as stating, "If we weren't still employing excellent people and pushing forward at full speed, it would be simple to slip behind and become some mediocre company."

So, which mindset do you have? Let's analyze twelve stunning distinctions between how rich individuals think and how poor or middle-class people think.

Rich Versus Poor Mindset

1. Rich people believe "I create my life." Poor mindsets think "life occurs to me."

If you want to generate money, it is vital that you feel that you are at the steering wheel of your life and that you create every moment of it, particularly your financial life. thereby taking responsibility for what's going on in their lives.

2. Rich people think big. The poor thing little.

We previously had a trainer lecturing at one of our seminars who went from a net worth of $250 thousand to over $600 million in under 3 years. When asked his secret, he answered, "Everything changed the day I started to think big."

Another method of comprehending this is to answer the following question: How many individuals do you serve or affect?

For instance, in my company, some trainers prefer speaking to groups of 20, some are happy with 100, others want an audience of 500, and yet others want 5000 people or more in attendance. There is a difference in pay between these trainers. You bet there is.

Who are you? How do you want to spend your life? How do you want to play the game?

Do you want to play in the big leagues or the small leagues, in the majors or the minors?

Will you play big or play small? It's your decision.

But hear this. It's not about you. It's about living your purpose. It's about living loyally to your mission. It's about contributing your piece of the puzzle to the world. It's about serving others.

Most of us are so locked in our egos that everything centers around "me, me, and more me." But again, it's not about you, it's about providing value to other people's lives. It's your decision. One way leads to being poor and sad, the other leads to money, purpose, and satisfaction.

It's time to quit hiding and start stepping out. It's time to stop needing and start leading. It's time to start becoming the star that you are.

3. Rich Mindsets Are Bigger Than Their Problems. Poor individuals are smaller than their troubles.

Getting rich is not a walk in the park. It's a voyage that is full of difficulties, twists, and diversions. The basic reality is that success is messy. The route is filled with peril, and that's why most people don't take it. They don't want the issues.

Therein lies one of the main disparities between rich people and poor people. Rich and successful individuals are greater than their difficulties, whereas poor and failed people are smaller than their troubles.

Poor individuals would do virtually everything to avoid anything that appeared like it might be a problem. They shy away from difficulties. The irony is that in their desire to make sure they don't have difficulties, they have the worst problem of all: they're poor and unhappy.

The answer to success is not to attempt to escape or diminish your issues; it's to develop yourself so you're greater than any difficulty.

It's simply an ordinary activity, like getting dressed or brushing your teeth. Whether you are rich or poor, playing big or playing little, difficulties do not go away. If you're breathing, you will always have so-called "problems."

What's vital to recognize is that the scale of the problem is never the true issue. What matters is the size of you! Remember, your money can only increase by the amount that you do! The aim is to develop yourself to a level where you can overcome any challenges that arise in your way of producing wealth and preserving it once you have it.

Rich individuals do not shy away from issues, do not avoid problems, and do not whine about problems. Rich individuals are financial fighters, and when a warrior is presented with a problem, they shout, "Bring it on!"

4. Rich People Focus on opportunities. Poor individuals concentrate on issues. Rich individuals sense an opportunity in every circumstance and try to explore it.

Rich mindsets sense potential development. Poor attitudes sense potential loss.

Rich mindsets concentrate on the rewards. Poor attitudes concentrate on the hazards.

We're not only talking about "positive thinking" here, we're talking about a habitual manner of perceiving the world. Fear is the source of poverty. Their thoughts are continuously searching for what's wrong or what may go wrong in every setting. Their primary mindset is "What if it doesn't work?" or, more frankly, "It won't work." Rich individuals, as we talked about before, take responsibility for building their lives and come from the mindset, "It will work because I'll make it work."

In the financial realm, like in most other domains, the risk is directly related to profit; usually, the bigger the benefit, the higher the risk. People with rich mentalities are ready to take that risk. They attempt to capitalize on opportunities even when they lack the necessary knowledge.

Rich people expect to succeed. They have trust in their talents, they have confidence in their inventiveness, and they feel that should the deal not be struck They can always get their money back or prosper in another manner. They search for methods to educate themselves so they are better equipped for the assignment.

On the other hand, impoverished people expect to fail. They lack confidence in themselves and their ability, and should things not work out, they fear it would be devastating.

You have to do something, purchase something, or start something to thrive financially. You have to recognize profit chances all around you instead of concentrating on methods of losing money. Rich mindsets always focus on a positive attitude.

Poor folks lack a cheerful mindset. "Poor" is a mindset. It is a lack of hope.

The difference between being broke and being poor is "mindset". The broke have little money right now but have a good attitude; they feel they can do better and can do better when they strive toward accomplishing something better. They think they're doomed to remain in poverty. The tiny guy can't get ahead. The poor are oppressed by the rich.

They can't save money because they think it will be stolen from them, and they spend money they do save or get as a windfall on pleasures because they don't think they can do better by doing anything else. For example, if you think you can't achieve better, you won't complete that tough degree program or take a second job to get out of debt since there is no reason.

Or they think they can't be affluent because they accept the fallacy that most billionaires inherited their money and status. The fact is that 80 percent of the rich are of the first generation, and fewer than 3 percent inherited enough to become millionaires.

A bad mindset might impede someone with even a decent salary. A typical instance is being terrified of investing, so you leave money in savings or CDs and earn less than the rate of inflation. Another is perceiving money as sinful, so they donate it to charity and "needy" friends and relatives.

They have nothing themselves, guaranteeing they have no money for their crises or retirement. This is why long-term financial success demands a healthy mental approach. Setbacks like unemployment or significant medical expenditures are recognized as transient and then dealt with.

5. Rich Mindsets Do Not Flaunt Their Wealth People with rich thinking conduct modest lifestyles.

The prevalent view of the rich is that they flaunt their money. We are lied to when they depict "the rich" wearing beautiful clothing, taking costly trips they boast about, and attending extravagant parties. In actuality, a very tiny fraction of the genuinely rich actually live this way, and most of those who do are high-income workers who have almost nothing saved.

Once the bonanza of a signing bonus or record deal is eaten up, they have nothing. Unfortunately, this image is perpetuated by marketing attempts to claim you have to spend money this way to get rich. Yet spending money on nice vehicles, lavish vacations, and other trappings of prosperity hinders you from doing so.

That constant $500 per month vehicle payment and the most expensive home you can afford will keep you from being wealthy. Most actual millionaires live in properties they can afford, and they prioritize paying off the mortgage. They own their automobiles for years and avoid car payments, although they may purchase a secondhand premium car and keep it running for 10 years.

They are pleased with what they have while they expand their enterprises and portfolios. And they earn their money honestly. There is a prevalent belief that most billionaires are liars and cheaters. One falsehood is that the rich don't pay their taxes, but the top 1 percent pays 40 percent of the taxes.

Another common misconception is that the wealthy are dishonest crooks who only became wealthy by causing harm to others.

In actuality, research reveals that the number one attribute of billionaires that they deem important to success is honesty. You can't continue in business if you're recognized for scamming people or getting sued for fraud all the time. You cannot form the quality connections that are essential to constructing a business network if you're a liar or cheat.

6. Rich mindsets understand the value of education. Poor mindsets are indifferent to the significance of ongoing learning or education.
Rich attitudes grow and upgrade their abilities throughout their lifetimes.
Education is a key driver of lifetime income. Note that this doesn't imply you have to go to an expensive private institution or acquire an advanced degree. However, you practically ensure that you'll be impoverished if you don't graduate high school.

One distinction between a rich and poor mindset is that the rich appreciate the importance of information. They're not part of the 40 percent of people who don't crack open a book after leaving high school. They're reading industry periodicals to learn more about their sector and thrive at work.

They're reading about money management and personal growth so that they achieve better in life. They're continuously learning. They'll ensure that they keep up their credentials, and they'll proactively pursue further certifications to qualify for increases and promotions.

7. Rich mindsets are better at risk management. Poor mindsets generally live in dread of taking new risks.

The rich aren't gambling with their money, whether it is taking vacations to the casinos or taking enormous chances with penny stocks. They are vigilant to control danger. One way they achieve this is by having the correct insurance coverage. They have life insurance, health insurance, and disability insurance so that a personal calamity doesn't wipe them or their families out. They won't simply start a company or venture without considering its profitability. They have emergency reserves with many months of savings so that they can meet a significant unexpected bill without having to go into debt. They emphasize protecting oneself before spending money on desires. This doesn't imply they don't invest in stocks or real estate. It indicates they do their studies before investing money.

They investigate the properties and the expenses to repair and sell them before they acquire them. They analyze equities or mutual funds before putting down their money. Educating yourself about numerous issues lessens your danger level. That is why one of the differences between rich and poor mindsets is that the poor typically live in fear of disaster, whereas the rich hope to weather the storm.

8. Rich versus Poor Mindset: Rich People Build Multiple Streams of Income. Poor folks have one source of income: their work.

Poor individuals put all of their eggs in one basket by being reliant on one source of income.

The affluent are famed for their work ethic, yet there are plenty of individuals who work hard but stay in poverty. There are various ways the rich function differently. One is that they take time to prepare for their financial future. They save for retirement so that they will have a passive source of income when they retire from their jobs.

They actively pay off debt and avoid taking on new debt so that their money goes further. They commit time to managing their money while investing every month, whether it is in a 401(k) or rental properties. If they own a company, they capitalize on it to earn more money.

It may be licensing intellectual property or renting out one of the apartments to earn extra cash. They may maintain a day job and yet educate or advise on the side to make extra cash. This may be a sort of risk management, too, as it offers them a head start if they lose their work or just wish to start their own full-time company.

9. Rich mindsets believe in saving, investing, and multiplying. Poor mindsets splurge on materialistic things. Poor folks end up saving nothing to invest.

Rich people save, save, save. They save 10% to 20% of their net income per year. The rich are deliberate. They don't put off saving for the future. They start saving with every paycheck, and they choose not to indulge so they can make that next 15 percent commitment to retirement.

They don't say they'll pay off the bill later. They design a strategy to pay off debt and implement it month after month until they're debt-free. According to "The Millionaire Next Door" and Chris Hogan's follow-up book "Everyday Millionaires", most millionaires by net worth either follow a budget or actively send a certain amount to savings and live off the remainder.

In short, they develop strategies and follow them. They make objectives, and by concentrating on them and consistently working toward them, they often attain them. Note that it isn't simply money. This is why the rich are less likely to be overweight, too. If you're already accustomed to routinely working toward financial objectives, an exercise and diet plan is simply one more plan to follow.

Remember, for anybody to cross the border from poverty to prosperity, they need to have a shift of mindset. If you want to grow rich, then you need to adjust your mindset and learn to perceive things from the perspective of the affluent.

Section III

Chapter 6

How To Stop Being Poor: Things you should consider doing if you want to break from the cycle of poverty

how to quit being poor. It seems like if you knew how to avoid being poor, you wouldn't be poor, right? It's not as straightforward as that. Breaking the poverty cycle requires time, work, and a lot of resolutions. With the appropriate actions, however, you can escape the poverty cycle and start living your greatest life.

However, it begins with knowing why you're poor. In this post, we'll examine the concrete methods you may learn to quit being poor and, in turn, put you on the road to financial health.

Realizing the terrible cycle of poverty is the first step in figuring out how to stop being poor. Before we explore how to get out of poverty, let's take a closer look at some of the causes that might be the root of your condition. Remember not to feel awful or embarrassed, but realize that sometimes it's due to situations that aren't in your control.

However, it is possible to earn your way out of the terrible cycle of poverty. Here are a few of the most prevalent reasons for poverty:

You come from an impoverished background. You've certainly heard the term "born with a silver spoon," right? It refers to people born into money or with all they need. Not everyone is as lucky, leaving them financially distressed from the outset.

Many individuals are born into low-income homes or families that lack ancestral wealth. If the practices of your ancestors persist in you, you might suffer from poverty too.

You've suffered tragic misfortune. Life is unexpected and occurs at the worst conceivable moments. Medical catastrophes, accidents, home fires, and criminal disasters may leave a family impoverished. No matter how much you prepare for the worst, reality has a strange way of working sometimes.

Medical bills frequently create financial troubles and even bankruptcy, whether from damage to your house or the inability to work due to a catastrophic injury. The crisis itself produces financial troubles, and then escaping the cycle of poverty seems practically impossible as you spin in circles attempting to get ahead of yourself.

Perhaps you've made terrible financial choices. Sometimes, to identify the reason we are impoverished, we need to look in the mirror. Our bad financial choices might have a cascading impact on our wealth. For example, if you develop the habit of using credit cards and living beyond your means, it may rapidly lead to poverty when you can't afford your expenses and the minimum payments on your credit cards.

If you've made terrible financial choices and caused yourself financial difficulty, it's not a time to blame yourself, but rather concentrate on what you can alter so you can learn how to quit being poor.

To break the terrible cycle of poverty, you need to start by acknowledging where you are. When you can admit you're suffering from poverty and need assistance, you'll be ready to follow these actions to quit being poor. For most individuals, riches, like fluency in another language, don't suddenly come to them one day. Getting rich demands persistent labor.

1. Focus on what you can control. Suffering from poverty seems overwhelming, but don't let it. Take control of how you feel and how you think about money. Rather than looking at the big picture and thinking, "I could never get out of this," look at the tiny things you can manage. For example, you can't control it when you become ill, but you can manage what you spend your money on outside of the basics.

When you're learning how to get out of poverty, you must concentrate on the controllable elements in your life. As you concentrate on them, you'll feel more confident in yourself and ready to take the most critical actions—the ones that will lead you out of poverty and also prevent getting sidetracked or distracted. And how do you know you are being distracted?...

How to Tell If You're Distracted Most individuals find it rather normal to be distracted. The bustle of ordinary life, heightened by social media and other forms of escape into a world that's not ours, has provided everyone with something to spend their time with.

Today, being distracted leads to squandering a substantial amount of time throughout the day. And calculatingly, "time equals money." Yet, it is not treated as seriously as it should be. If you can detect the indications of distraction, then you can confront the problem in time and live the life you want to.

"Most individuals don't want to recognize the difficult fact that diversion is always a harmful escape from reality."

We have grown so accustomed to being distracted that we scarcely view it as a negative thing anymore. Distraction may appear differently to different people. However, if you want to become in-distractable, here are some symptoms to look out for to determine whether you're being distracted and solve the problem as soon as possible.

You find yourself wanting to check your phone frequently. Checking your phone regularly or feeling the urge to continually be active on social media during work hours or while you're executing a job is one of the greatest indications of distraction. You gaze at a thing for a long time, unable to figure out what to do with it. Although you have something to accomplish and the resources to do it with, you find it hard to figure out how to go about the work. The stuff you're working on seems so dull that you want to do something fun. This originates from your unhappiness with the job you're doing. This discontent leads to you feeling bored with your work and seeking external consolation in something fun. When you're doing something boring, you're thinking about doing the things you like: Constantly thinking about things you enjoy is what most individuals do when they cannot maintain traction with the job in front of them. This frequently happens when they are thinking of things they want to do after the work is done. Audio-visual stimulation surrounding you makes it hard to concentrate on the work at hand. Although you're focusing on the job, every speech or passing picture attracts your attention. This may induce you to forget about work and listen in on a nearby chat instead.

When we talk about distractions, we're talking about human behavior and responses to the distractions themselves. And every human action is characterized by

- **External or**
- **Internal stimuli.**

External stimulus. These external cues compete for our attention with whatever task we're ultimately attempting to concentrate on. Sometimes, the simple existence of an item itself, such as having your phone nearby, might inspire you to pay attention to it.

Internal stimulus. There is also internal stimulus, which is simply indications that originate from inside, such as hunger, concern about an approaching event, or feeling chilly.
All human activity is triggered by external or internal impulses; consequently, traction and distraction both come from the same source.

How to Overcome Distraction and Become "un-distractable" Distractions may quickly take over your life, but here I detail Seven easy strategies to take back your power and become un-distractable. how to control your attention and choose your life.

demonstrated methodologies for conquering distractions The most productive individuals in the world accomplish one thing at a time. We've all been there. Indeed, even with good motivations to keep focused, we discover ourselves looking at virtual entertainment when we ought to be chipping away at a venture. We can't resist the urge to snatch our wireless the second we hear a warning. And afterward, there's email! In the event that we aren't checking it like clockwork, we stress that we could miss something significant.

Distractions can appear to be difficult to keep away from. Measurements show that distractions cause a gigantic loss in efficiency. The regular supervisor is intruded on like clockwork, and workers for the most part invest 28% of their energy managing superfluous interferences and attempting to refocus.

Anyway, how might you assume command over your time and consideration? The following are seven demonstrated systems for beating distractions and recovering your concentration.

I) Put yourself in no distraction mode. Start building propensities that assist you with killing distractions and keeping on track. Begin by establishing a climate wherein you're less enticed to get distracted by some different option from what you're chipping away at. This is generally difficult to do. As far as one might be concerned, a significant number of us depend on a PC to take care of our responsibilities; however, we likewise find our greatest distractions empowered by the utilization of a PC on the Web. If you frequently end up meandering over to video or shopping sites, consider utilizing a site blocker application.

Work to develop propensities that signal to yourself and the people around you that you're in distraction-free mode. Close the road to your office. Put on sound-blocking earphones. Switch off your telephone or put it on quiet and move it away from you (so you can only get it with significant effort). On the off chance that you work in an open office, you might find it supportive to move to a calmer area. Investigations have discovered that distractions happen 64 percent more frequently in an open office, and we're intruded on by others all the more frequently in that climate too.

Remove as many reasons and distractions as possible so that you can devote your full attention to each task in turn—no multitasking.

II) Set three primary targets consistently. An extensive rundown of activities can seem inconceivable and leave us feeling overpowered. We're prepared to surrender before we start, and that is the point at which it turns out to not be difficult to yield to distractions. You can counterbalance this by giving yourself three goals to achieve consistently. Keep in touch with them on a tacky note and post it where you can see it each time you gaze upward from your work.

By restricting the number of day-to-day objectives, you'll have clearly defined what you really want to chip away at. You'll work with a more prominent expectation on those undertakings, and your psyche will be less well-suited to wander.

Ask yourself each day: What are the three most significant things to achieve today? Some other errands ought to be placed on a different plan for the day. When you've completed the first three objectives, you can begin to handle the minor errands.

III) Give yourself a more limited time. More hours worked do not imply that you get more things done. That's what parkinson's regulation says "work will, in general, grow to occupy the time we have accessible for its finish." And, in general, we spend our time avoiding distractions. This is because our psyche is wired to preserve energy whenever the situation allows. In the event that we don't need to follow through with something, there's a decent opportunity we will not make it happen. All things being equal, we'll permit ourselves to get sucked into a YouTube video or a game application on our telephone.

However, when we have a deadline, we unexpectedly foster extreme concentration and avoid distractions at all costs. At the point when you realize you need to finish something, you'll sort out a method for getting it done.

To take out distractions, give yourself a more limited time span to complete your work. This resembles giving yourself a counterfeit cutoff time, however, upheld by something that considers you responsible. Tell your chief or client that you'll provide them with a draft of an undertaking before the day's over. Find a responsible accomplice who will hold you to your objective period of time. Setting a hard cutoff time, however, you do it, will help you avoid distractions and increase your efficiency.

IV). Screen your brain's meandering. We spend almost 50% of our waking time contemplating some different options from what we should do, as per one Harvard study. We are moving along automatically, and our brain is meandering to a limited extent to keep away from the work of zeroing in on something. The key to increased efficiency is recognizing when your brain is distracted and welcoming your attention back to the task at hand.
This implies focusing on your viewpoints and recognizing when your psyche begins floating. This permits you to oversee what you center around and divert your considerations when you goof. Rather than

permitting yourself to continue to wander over to web-based entertainment to look at your newsfeed, you effectively put the brakes on this distraction.

Concentrate on which distractions are particularly difficult to avoid so that you can overcome them sooner. At the point when you feel a craving to yield to a distraction, calmly inhale and intentionally decide not to respond to it. Whenever you've surrendered and permitted yourself to zero in on something different, such as understanding messages, it's harder to refocus and take your consideration back to the main job.

To put it plainly, be aware of your viewpoints rather than permitting yourself to skip between assignment and distraction.

V) Train your brain by making a game out of it. Your brain resembles a muscle; to utilize it, you really want to develop it. We really want to prepare our brain to keep on track by slowly dealing with our fixation.

This will reinforce our capacity to concentrate for longer periods of time.

An extraordinary method for starting to do this is through the "Clockwork Technique," in which you set a clock and are totally centered around an undertaking for a while, like 45 minutes in a row. Then, at that point, permit yourself a 15-minute break.

On the off chance that 45 minutes is a stretch, begin with something more reasonable, like 25 minutes, and afterward, offer yourself a five-minute reprieve. The thought is to make a round of it, to challenge yourself to work determinedly on your undertaking until the clock rings. Then, at that point, permit yourself to glut on any distraction you need, yet only for a designated time frame.

It has returned to work after the break until the clock strikes 12. You'll be astonished by the amount you can complete using this strategy!

IV) Take on really challenging work. Assuming you're experiencing difficulty centering and are constantly occupied, it is possible that your work isn't drawing you in completely. You could feel like you're really buckling down the entire day, yet it may be the case that your brain is battling weariness and hoping to occupy the time with something seriously fascinating.

Complex undertakings request a greater amount of our functioning memory and consideration, meaning we have less intellectual ability staying to meander to the closest invigorating distraction. We're probably going to go into a condition of all-out work submersion when our capacities are tested. We get exhausted when our abilities extraordinarily surpass the requests of our work, for example, when we do thoughtless information passage for a few hours.

Evaluate the degree of unproductive busy work you're doing. Might it be said that you are struggling with taking part in the undertaking? This could show that you have the ability to take on additional difficult ventures. At the point when we take on more complicated work that pushes our expertise and scholarly cutoff points, we can become consumed and hyper-focused on the assignment. Our brains are wired to zero in on anything that is novel, pleasurable, or undermining. What's more, handling these errands provides us with pride.

We have no such feeling of achievement with an undertaking we consider humble.

VII) Break the pattern of pressure and distraction. Stress can likewise play a significant role in our failure to concentrate or defeat distractions. Time and again, we end up attempting to work while feeling overpowered. This leaves us fatigued and depleted, quickly drawn off track, and incapable of focusing. Assuming you're quickly flustered, it can show that you're under increased pressure.

There's even a name for it: "quickly flustered uneasiness." Side effects include:
You experience issues concentrating, and your brain continually floats away from what you were zeroing in on. You have more trouble framing considerations and keeping focused than is typical. Your reasoning feels obfuscated and weakened. You feel your transient memory is disappointing, as it typically is. Managing your stress will assist you in regaining your concentration and overcoming distractions with ease. You should track down ways of quieting your psyche and loosening up your body to lessen the body's pressure reaction. ensure you get sufficient rest. Work on breathing activities and track down ways of containing your nervousness.

2. Avoid Toxic Relationship:
Anything can harm your finances if you let it. Sure, a toxic relationship could harm your finances. It could cause you to make poor financial choices. A relationship where there is too much spending can crash your path to wealth and success. Apart from other negative issues of toxic relationships like feelings of low self-worth, helplessness, fear, anxiety, depression, insecurity, paranoia, and even narcissism, which have a bad effect on your health, a toxic relationship can cause you a financial crash.

In a relationship where there is overspending, recklessly spending on shopping, travel, or eating out to the extent that it affects the other partner is the number one reason for financial stress. According to a survey conducted by ET Wealth, 41.4% of respondents said they fought because of their own or their partner's spending habits. If your partner's spending habits are pushing you into debt and affecting your own savings plan, it is time to bring in change. Also, if one of the partners is lying about money, it's another red light. Lying about spending or hiding an addiction such as gambling are other big red flags. Not being open I'm not choosing anything for anyone, but your partner should be someone with the same mindset as you towards wealth. Discuss the difference with your partner, and if the issue is proving difficult, the only remedial measure is to come clean with your partner if you know what you are pursuing. Don't let a toxic relationship tie you down.

3. As a crucial first step in overcoming poverty, stop comparing yourself to others. Quit feeling envious of your siblings, friends, or neighbors' possessions if you want to learn how to stop being poor. Don't let your possessions determine your value. What does it matter if your neighbor has a Mercedes and you have a Toyota? Will driving a more luxurious vehicle make them

like you more? In such cases, they aren't really buddies.

Prioritize your thoughts above those of others. If all of your family and friends purchase name-brand products, but you are quite content with the less costly generic products, you should proceed as necessary.

You don't know other people's financial situations, so don't strive to stay up with them. Sure, they could seem to be able to afford the pricey clothes or fine meals, but how can you be sure that they aren't running up credit card debt that they can't afford?,
Concentrate only on you. Great if other people like you. They don't belong in your life if they reject you because you don't spend as much money as they do or own the same possessions.

4. Surround yourself with people who make wise financial judgments. Does the thought that you are the average of the five people

you spend the most time with terrify you?, Consider the people you interact with the most. Do they manage their money well or do they spend it carelessly?

There's a good chance that you'll unconsciously follow their lead. Even while you could claim to want to learn how to quit being poor, your behavior when you're in your "group" suggests otherwise. Rather, surround yourself with individuals who share your values.

Subconsciously, you will make wise financial judgments if you are among individuals who do. You won't feel overwhelmed when you escape the cycle of poverty since you'll automatically make sensible financial choices.

5. Create a strategy to end your poverty by assessing your current situation. You must be aware of your situation in order to understand how to quit being impoverished. Being honest with oneself makes this stage

difficult. You must assess your financial situation by looking at your bank accounts and comparing them to your obligations.

Knowing your situation can help you make better future plans. Make a budget right away if you don't have one already. Track your financial intake and outflow to see where adjustments need to be made using an app, paper and ink, or an Excel spreadsheet.

Do you spend more money than you bring in? Is it too difficult to pay your expenses on time each month? Sort your expenditures into categories, decide where you can make savings, and take it one step at a time.

Be kind to yourself throughout this period. You're going to make errors, and that's alright. Pick up the pieces so you can go on and learn from them. so that you may start saving money and stop living paycheck to paycheck.

6. Establish objectives to advance financially Without objectives, you cannot escape poverty. You must demonstrate your desire to improve your circumstances. Make your objectives visible, if you haven't done so before. Sticky notes with these reminders should be placed on your refrigerator and bathroom mirror, two locations where you will see them every day.

If you have artistic ability, make a vision board and display it prominently in your house. When you are no longer in poverty, what will you do? What are your objectives? Do you wish to discover your ideal career, get a new vehicle, or buy a home? Your objectives should be as detailed as you can make them in order to inspire you to put in the necessary effort to end the cycle of poverty.

7. Begin a second business to boost your income. If your 9-to-5 income is insufficient

but a part-time job sounds taxing, think about starting a side business. Anyone can establish a side business from home, and because you decide when you work on them, you can even manage multiple ones. Freelance writing, survey-taking, graphic design, or driving for Uber are all examples of side businesses.

Companies like Uber, DoorDash, and Instacart make it simple to work outside the home without having defined hours or a manager hovering over your shoulder. Platforms like Fiverr and Upwork also make it simple to work from home. Set aside a portion of the money you earn from a side job for specified costs that will enable you to escape poverty.

8. Invest your time in furthering your education and job development. Did you know that investing in yourself is one of the best investments you can make? Starting with you, you can learn how to quit being

poor. You may improve your profession without spending a lot of money on yourself. It's just about timing sometimes.

Many businesses offer possibilities to further your education or free tuition help. You must look for and seize the possibilities that present themselves. Everyone must begin somewhere, even if they are starting from scratch.

Just take a look at Michael Jordan; despite being cut from his high school team, look at everything that he managed to achieve. Make an investment in yourself by making time to educate yourself and advance your profession.

9. Manage your money well and make savings where you can. Therefore, if you don't control your spending, you can't break the cycle of poverty. Making progress requires a budget, but you also need to keep an eye on your expenditures. If you are a

compulsive shopper, get an accountability partner—someone you must explain your purchases to too—to help you stay on track.

When you have someone who will challenge you and demand sincere responses, you may hesitate before making an impulsive purchase. This is not to say that you can't spend money; everyone must do so sometimes. However, the secret to eradicating poverty is understanding where and how to spend money.

10. Reduce your debt to put yourself on the road to financial stability. Only by being able to reduce your debt will you be able to escape the cycle of poverty. Any alternative use of your money would come at the opportunity cost of high-interest credit card debt. Create a plan that will enable you to pay off your debt as quickly as feasible.

Even if you are only able to pay an additional $10 a month toward your debt, that $10 will be deducted off the main sum, which will prevent interest from accruing. Apply the debt snowball strategy to reduce your debt.

Sort your debts from lowest to highest according to their balance. Pay the lowest debt (first in line) the minimum amount due on each loan, then make any additional payments you can. Continue doing this until the initial loan is fully paid off.

Next, increase the minimum payment of the subsequent loan by the amount you paid toward the first debt (the minimum payment plus any extra). The snowball effect helps you get rid of high-interest debt.

11. Make as much leeway in your budget for savings as you can, and invest and save as much as you can. 20% of your budget should be set aside for savings and debt repayment, but because you're seeking to end your cycle of poverty, this may not be realistic.

As you go, try to save a larger amount of money each month. In an ideal world, you'd have three to six months' worth of expenses saved up so you could avoid experiencing this again. Just concentrate on setting aside your first $1,000 if you are just getting started. You might make plans to save additional money after you arrive.

You may discover how to escape poverty by using these strategies to assist you. It is not as difficult as it may appear to learn how to escape poverty. It requires commitment, endurance, and a great deal of grace. You're going to make errors, and that's alright. Don't wallow in it; pick up the pieces

The lifestyle modifications listed below have helped self-made millionaires and billionaires succeed and may do the same for you.

I. Throw out your regular paycheck. Rich individuals often work for themselves, whereas regular people choose jobs with more security. Not that there aren't world-class performers who clock in and out for a living, but for the most part, this is the riskiest and slowest route to success. "The exceptional ones are aware that entrepreneurship is the surest path to prosperity."

That is not to say that you should immediately leave your day job. Self-made billionaire Daymond John, who survived on the tips he earned waiting tables at Red Lobster while developing the clothing business that would eventually become a $6 billion brand, believes the notion that you must leave your 9-to-5 job to become a successful entrepreneur "is nonsense."

II. Learn to tolerate discomfort. World-class thinkers realize early on that being a billionaire isn't simple, and the urge for comfort may be fatal. To make more money or advance in life, you must be ready to move outside of your comfort zone. "They develop the ability to function in a constant condition of uncertainty."

Leaving your comfort zone may include choosing a job that you don't feel qualified for, learning a new skill, or asking for advice from others. After all, cold calling was how self-made billionaire Bobbi Brown and businessman Koel Thomae began their respective successful careers.

III. make salary concessions Negotiating may be difficult, but failing to be paid what you're worth might mean the difference between living a wealthy or ordinary life.

The amount of money you are paid now, after all, "is the number one element that will influence your future earning potential and bring you to $1 million the quickest," according to self-made billionaire Grant Sabatier.

Be prepared before requesting a raise. Read up on career advice, negotiation advice, and costly negotiation mistakes.

IV. Don't brag; just show up. waited until your companies and assets were generating many reliable streams of income before you purchased your first fancy watch or automobile. Monetize those your luxuries for the main time, use that money and invest on something one or two more times. You will be glad with your outcome.

V. Be prepared to spend money borrowed from others. Rich folks aren't shy about asking for money. They continue to utilize other people's money to make it happen if they have a wonderful concept but are unable to afford it.
Rich people are aware that their personal inability to afford something is irrelevant. Is this something worth purchasing, investing in, or pursuing? If this is the case, affluent individuals are aware that money is always

accessible since they are always hunting for successful investments and top performers to make those investments.

VI. Take chances and be prepared to make errors. Marcus Lemonis, a self-made billionaire and the presenter of CNBC's "The Profit," claims that too many individuals allow fear to prevent them from taking critical choices.

You will fail sometimes. Who cares? Consider every opportunity as a chance to pick up new abilities, rather than being afraid to take chances.

The typical mind tends to think about investing.

Richard Branson, a self-made millionaire, states, "Nobody ever completes a task perfectly the first time. You need to swiftly learn from your failures in business since it's like playing a huge game of chess. "Entrepreneurs that are successful don't fear failure; instead, they learn from it and go on."

SUMMARY

It is not as difficult as it may seem to learn how to escape poverty. It requires commitment, endurance, and a great deal of grace. You're going to make errors, and that's alright. Don't wallow in it; pick up the pieces and move on.

You can escape the cycle of poverty once and for all if you move slowly and forward as much as you can despite the occasional backward steps you're bound to take.

In the Start to Build a Solid Foundation bundle, you can take charge of your finances and learn how to change your mindset, set goals, and find the best budget for you. You must stop judging money by what it can buy if you want to be a member of the wealthy elite.

Does it really matter what the wealthy think? ...Yes, if you want to become wealthy as well. By literally following someone or a route, you can reach your destination. if you've finished reading this book already. It seems to be what you think at this point. What steps and actions are you prepared to take going forward? You are free to go either way. Choose between becoming and remaining wealthy or remaining the straightforward, average person you are.

If you aren't working on it, it doesn't matter how wealthy you are. As time passes, you will only reach your lowest point. Learn how to become and remain wealthy with the help of this book. You can learn how to escape poverty by using these steps to help you.

What else would you like to improve to achieve your goal? Go on, make your dream happen.

www.ingramcontent.com/pod-product-compliance
Lightning Source LLC
Chambersburg PA
CBHW051537240526
45465CB00027B/601